Sunday Double Suicide

SUNDAY DOUBLE SUICIDE

GORO TAKANO

BLAZEVOX[BOOKS]

Buffalo, New York

Interior design and typesetting by Geoffrey Gatza
Cover Artist: Yu Shiotsuki

First Edition
ISBN: 978-1-60964-394-2
Library of Congress Control Number: 2021952025

BlazeVOX [books]
131 Euclid Ave
Kenmore, NY 14217
Editor@blazevox.org

publisher of weird little books

BlazeVOX [books]

blazevox.org

21 20 19 18 17 16 15 14 13 12 01 02 03 04 05 06 07 08 09 10 11

BlazeVOX

Contents

SUNDAY DOUBLE SUICIDE

Face Masks and a Stick

I still leave this door open all the time, because I want this space to be your final hideout
"WE'VE LOST EVERYTHING — EVEN THIS BLUE SKY IS NOT OURS ANYMORE"
None of you have come here yet, but I will not stop waiting alone with the door unlocked
"NO USE ESCAPING — BLOCKADING ALL THE BORDERS IS NOW POINTLESS"

"WE'VE LOST EVERYTHING — EVEN THIS BLUE SKY IS NOT OURS ANYMORE"
Only with this stick in my grasp, I can keep chasing that devil full speed even in the dark
"NO USE ESCAPING — BLOCKADING ALL THE BORDERS IS NOW POINTLESS"
While you all are yet frightened within the borders, I will fight against it on your behalf

Only with this stick in my grasp, I can keep chasing that devil full speed even in the dark
"WHO CAN DEBUNK THAT INVISIBLE THING RUNNING RIOT INCESSANTLY?"
While you all are yet frightened within the borders, I will fight against it on your behalf
"LET'S RELAX HERE WITH OUR MASKS ON WHILE HE KILLS IT THERE FOR US"

"WHO CAN DEBUNK THAT INVISIBLE THING RUNNING RIOT INCESSANTLY?"
Before starting the fight, I must question that creature whether it has a human soul or not
"LET'S RELAX HERE WITH OUR MASKS ON WHILE HE KILLS IT THERE FOR US"
If its answer is no, I will kill it immediately — if its answer is yes, well, I must pardon it

Before starting the fight, I must question that creature whether it has a human soul or not
"IF HE CANNOT KILL IT, IT WILL SIMPLY MEAN OUR RUIN — IF HE CAN,"
If its answer is no, I will kill it immediately — if its answer is yes, well, I must pardon it
"WE'LL SEE HIM FIRST AS A HERO, AND THEN EXECUTE HIM AS A MADMAN"

"IF HE CANNOT KILL IT, IT WILL SIMPLY MEAN OUR RUIN — IF HE CAN,"
I posed the question to it, but it didn't respond at all. So I clubbed it to death with this stick
"WE'LL SEE HIM FIRST AS A HERO, AND THEN EXECUTE HIM AS A MADMAN"
Now I'm sure limitless tranquility will be back shortly. Neither beginning nor end will exist

I posed the question to it, but it didn't respond at all. So I clubbed it to death with this stick
"IF WE FORGIVE HIS SINFUL ACT OF POSING AS OUR SPOKESMAN OR PATRIOT"
Now I'm sure limitless tranquility will be back shortly. Neither beginning nor end will exist
"EVEN WE'LL BE MISTAKEN FOR THE FIRM BELIEVERS IN HIS ODD EUGENICS"

"IF WE FORGIVE HIS SINFUL ACT OF POSING AS OUR SPOKESMAN OR PATRIOT"
I killed it as a man in charge of punishing every illegal stay. I cleansed its dead face, though
"EVEN WE'LL BE MISTAKEN FOR THE FIRM BELIEVERS IN HIS ODD EUGENICS"
As to those who suffer grief at its death, I will do my very best to heal their emotional pain

I killed it as a man in charge of punishing every illegal stay. I cleansed its dead face, though
"EVEN IF THE NEWS OF HIS KILLING IS MERELY FALSE OR SIMPLY BASELESS"
As to those who suffer grief at its death, I will do my very best to heal their emotional pain
"OUR EXECUTION WILL SATISFY HIM, BECAUSE HE CAN END UP A SOCRATES"

"EVEN IF THE NEWS OF HIS KILLING IS MERELY FALSE OR SIMPLY BASELESS"
Why do you hire illegal persons and have them wait in line to get luxury items in your place?
"OUR EXECUTION WILL SATISFY HIM, BECAUSE HE CAN END UP A SOCRATES"
Why do you try to kill me, doubting my sincere inquiry about the presence of a human soul?

Why do you hire illegal persons and have them wait in line to get luxury items in your place?
"IF THE FALL OF THE INVISIBLE DEVIL IS A FLAT LIE — WHAT IF IT TRIES TO"
Why do you try to kill me, doubting my sincere inquiry about the presence of a human soul?
"CONNECT WITH US AGAIN, LIKE A CHERRY BLOOM GRAFTED TO MULTIPLY?"

"IF THE FALL OF THE INVISIBLE DEVIL IS A FLAT LIE — WHAT IF IT TRIES TO"

Am I the poorest victim in this case? Am I identical to the devil? Do you have human souls?

"CONNECT WITH US AGAIN, LIKE A CHERRY BLOOM GRAFTED TO MULTIPLY?"

Did it return "yes" to my question through its silence? Did my stick get its response wrong?

Am I the poorest victim in this case? Am I identical to the devil? Do you have human souls?

"IF SO, SHALL WE SUCK HIS BLOOD AFTER HIS END TO ACQUIRE IMMUNITY?"

Did it return "yes" to my question through its silence? Did my stick get its response wrong?

"GOOD AND EVIL WILL SLIP OUR MIND! ONLY NOTHINGNESS WILL MATTER!"

"IF SO, SHALL WE SUCK HIS BLOOD AFTER HIS END TO ACQUIRE IMMUNITY?"

I still leave this door open all the time, because I want this space to be your final hideout

"GOOD AND EVIL WILL SLIP OUR MIND! ONLY NOTHINGNESS WILL MATTER!"

None of you have come here yet, but I will not stop waiting alone with the door unlocked

Caterpillar

On a summer day, in the shade of a tree, a man gives a bouquet to a woman. "With my deepest love," he adds, whereas she says to herself: "Another liar." She never ceases to show him a bogus enchanting smile, however. He rubs his sole against the asphalt road to scrape the carcass of a butterfly from it. After the rendezvous the woman departs from the main street flooded with old love songs and comes back to her room where nobody awaits her return. She whispers: "Listen to me now, the whole world! If you like to call this space helplessly loveless, do as you like!" Laughing loudly, she stares at the bouquet again. "It should not be to blame for anything." The woman pours water into a vase and arranges the victim of human love in it, when she notices a pure green caterpillar on one of the petals, wriggling subtly as if it is fidgeting while anticipating something. "Ah, probably, that lewd man is longing to watch nothing but my naked body wriggling this way under him – he doesn't know that carefully hidden in the present he had carefully chosen was a worm-shaped copy of my true self — wait — doesn't he, really? — what if he selected intentionally this bouquet with this caterpillar on it?" The more complex love turns in her head, the more profound it looks in her eyes. She laughs again and picks up the worm with her fingers. Landing safely on her bare breast, it shrinks faintly while the woman casts a motherly quiet glance at its back. Midnight — while she hums one of the old love songs she heard on the main street, the worm keeps crawling around her heart. The phantom of a butterfly slips from her room and flies silently through a window. It keeps riding the strong wind, making its way through the sheer darkness, and, finally, at a loss how to get back to where it once belonged, strays into the shade of a tree where another sole is awaiting its death.

Jokes

Monday --- unexpectedly
By express delivery
Someone's heart arrived in my house
The sender's name was totally unfamiliar
Scribbled on the enclosed short letter was
Only this: "To a verbose aphasic man"
I joked: "Sent from a ghost or something?"
The delivery man said with a smile:
"Reconstruction has been almost finished in this area
So we have no more ghosts, perhaps"

Tuesday --- I took out the heart out of the box
It quickly swelled and swelled and
Ended up a mansion with many doors
I opened one of the doors and went in
A woman was sewing alone and her varied threads
Slowly assembled and changed into lovely flowers
The surrounding of each flower turned black
The thicker the blackness the more radiant the flowers
She muttered: "Everything has been motionless since then"

Wednesday --- I opened the next door on a whim
Someone yelled suddenly from within: "You again?"
I said: "I've never seen you before, sir"
The voice: "Ha? You came here yesterday
Didn't you say you're working for a company
Assisting suicide wishers for population control?"
My swift denial was drowned out by another yell:
"Change yourself first if you want to change the world!"

Thursday --- the dweller of the next door said:
"I know you're the notorious villain on the run
You deceived one single woman after another
And made them all pregnant so that
Our future government can obtain more taxpayers!"

My immediate denial was unheard again
I hastened to go out to find neither past nor future
Waiting for me on an endlessly straight corridor
I felt as if I had kept playing hide-and-seek
For a long time only with a single stranger

Friday --- a line on the door I had not opened yet
Solemnly read: "TORTURER WANTED"
As soon as I opened the door slowly
An automatic message slid into the unmanned room:
"Neither past experience nor language proficiency needed
Daily wage: $100 --- nine to five --- no overtime work
Your fundamental human rights and freedom are
Not a little limited" --- I heard a painful moan of a woman
Coming from behind the wall --- it carried me away
Another voice from the corridor: "All are dead here"

Saturday --- while retracing the corridor alone
I joked to myself: "Death is not a goodbye but a feast! ---
If you grow without knowing the meaning of the word
'Death' --- you can surely turn immortal!"
Suddenly I was arrested and taken to the eyesight test room
Set before me was a picture of variously-colored circles
Some big and some small --- overlapping with one another
I was asked to say what I could see in them
I showed a passing fancy: "A flower, perhaps?"
Torture started and made me moribund

Without adjusting fully to the atmosphere of the mansion
I finally came back home with bruises all over
I saw the delivery again and found myself little by little losing
Verboseness --- I joked to myself again: "Am I like a ghost now?"
And began to worry --- is today really Sunday?

Why Don't We Meet Again A Hundred Years Later?

Today I decided to dump my old backpack
The one I kept using for so many years
Its sky-blue surface is bruised here and there
It doesn't seem to fit me as easily as before
My deceased wife bought it for me
On her deathbed she stared at it on my back
And said: "After I disappear, you may become
Something like a vanquished country in war"
I still remember her distorted face

The very first book I put into this backpack was
The pocketbook version of *The Old Man and the Sea*
I bought it for my son's birthday --- despite my wish
He gave it the cold shoulder --- now its dusty cover
Stays on his shelf, while Santiago's long dream and
A phantom of the marlin's bones stay in the backpack

After my wife's funeral, I put into this backpack
Her Buddhist memorial tablet and carried it around
My son said to me: "The dead are far easier to carry
Than the living" --- every time I took out the tablet and put it back
Into the backpack, I felt as if I were a professional magician

When my son met with a serious accident
I rushed to his hospital with this backpack on
I mopped my eyes knowing his life was in no danger
I put into the backpack his dirtied clothes and
Brought them home --- his body odor oozing
From them met with the fishy stench of death
And the old fisherman's solitude --- the three got
Tangled up like laundry in a washing machine

The last book I put into this backpack was about
A blue-eyed soldier whose country has been colonized
He pledges allegiance to the foreign colonizers' army
And dies a martyr without his conquerors noticing

No colonist praises his "patriotism" until his death

I haven't finished reading this epic story yet
But I read repeatedly the poem written by the soldier protagonist
During his service --- its title is "Why Don't We Meet Again
A Hundred Years Later?" --- the blue-eyed man puts it into his
Old backpack and carries it around until the last day of his life
Strangely, the poem suggests that he has no intention to
Be a "patriot" at all --- I wonder whom he wants to meet again
A hundred years later --- under what circumstances?
The mystery will be solved in the pages I'll read from now

When I was about to dump the old backpack into a bin
My son stopped me and said: "I will use it from now"
I asked him why, but he merely showed me a shy smile
Strangely, the backpack on his back made me imagine
Seismic waves of people celebrating their own emancipation
I said: "The older I get, the more I lose"
The son's reply amazed me with its unexpected maturity:
"In the near future, Dad, a woman like Mom will appear
In front of you and buy you a much better backpack"

The son swept out and, in solitude, I started falling
Again into the vision of a landscape a hundred years
From now --- as Santiago maybe does in his last moments

Stare-and-make-laugh Game

Without being noticed by anyone
a cicada falls straight to the ground
While thrashing its wings in vain
the insect is slowly drawn to death

Its eyes seem to show the revival
of the memory of flitting in the sky
and shrilling wherever it visited
but there is no knowing their truth

A human shadow stops by and looks
down on the quietness intensifying
in the insect lying on its back as if
to start a stare-and-make-laugh game

The shadow makes different funny
faces as it asks silently: "Why must
I hear a big chorus of 'Be a mother'
everyday though I want no children?

No true solidarity is possible without
revering solitude --- is it a wrong idea?"
The cicada's droll face wins the game
for its opponent cannot stifle a laugh

Smelling out another imminent death
an army of ants begins a quick march
Another human shadow squats before
the dying bug and watches it with scorn

"I hate your shrieks --- you're a nuisance
for us humans like my parents' generation
I was one of the victims of their shrieks!"
The shadow starts making a funny face

The shadow's monologue goes on: "I met
my parents for the last time through glass
They were too senile to recognize me ---
they only shrieked: 'We might've killed!'

They took the glass between me and them
for me and called my name to it --- maybe
they even believed a thing like you is me"
The shadow gets bored with the death and

walks off --- the cicada's eyeballs see off
the lonesome back as its carcass is slowly
enclosed by the ants --- they halt for a split
second as if to bow just as medical students

do before a human body donated for their
autopsy practice --- the dead bug's guts are
slowly eaten and its eyes reflect the sunset
Another shadow watches it sympathetically

"Are you also a loser of bitter competition?"
The shadow repeats so without showing
any interest in starting another facial game
"No live cicada is shrieking for you now!"

Wetting the two tiny eyeballs may be either
a teardrop or a raindrop --- the sun goes down
in the rain --- no human shadows --- no more
ants --- cicadae cry no more in the darkness

Deserted here are the clownish eyeballs only
Something is in operation over those spheres
As if to endeavor to make this unknown thing
laugh eternally --- another staring game begins

Mower

Long time ago — the first time you were taught
        in your junior-high-level ESL class
The grammatical difference between the active voice
        and the passive one
You were somehow recalling a strange woman
        you had met by chance a while before
Without listening intently to
        the earnest lecture of your male teacher

The only overpopulated city in your nation is
        right here
The only section overgrown with weeds in this city is
        the place where you saw the woman working alone
She was mowing weeds with a sharp sickle
        in the middle of the quiet empty lot
Placed near her feet was a bulky rusty copper plate
        on which a man's face was engraved

The first time you met the woman on your way home
        from the school ended up your last time
You stopped to watch silently her strenuous mowing
        and she made a brief pause to look at you
She stomped the copper plate barefoot several times
        and yelled at you: "In no time at all
The souls of our ancestors will return here — so
        somebody must clean this place now"

"The souls of ancestors? Is there any tomb here?" —
        she ignored your question
Her enigmatic smile looked
        simultaneously young and old
She added: "Am I really mowing the weeds? Or —
        are the weeds mowing themselves?
Or — am I mowing myself? Oh my —
        now I'm terribly confused!"

"There are only two types of voices in the world of language
          — passive and active"
The male teacher stressed several times and wrote down
          two short sentences on the blackboard:
"You are controlled" and "You controlled" — he added:
          "Which is the accurate passive-voice form?
The former one, okay? You need the linking verb in this case and
          this be-verb originally embodies EXISTENCE!"

As soon as she finished a day's share of mowing
          the woman turned to the evening glow and
Began to confuse you again: "I used to make countless scarecrows
          — all handmade and completely humanlike —
To protect this sanctuary from harmful beasts and birds"
          "Any crop to protect from them in this weedy place?"
She ignored your question again and added:
          "Did I make scarecrows? Did they make themselves?

Or — did I make myself? — aren't you
          one of the scarecrows I made long time ago?"
The English class was ending — you said to yourself:
          "If I were a scarecrow, so would everyone else"
The woman stared at the man on the copper plate and said:
          "Because this guy loved me too much
He begged me to tread on his face barefoot every day and night
          even after his death"

The engraved man looked in your eyes like
          simultaneously yourself and a god

Several years after you had been taught
          the passive voice for the first time
The "No Trespassing" sign was set on the empty lot
          by order of the public office
The whole weedy place was fenced with barbed wire
          and you heard through the grapevine
The strange woman had been officially labeled as a "menace"
          and forcibly ejected by the authorities

You shook hands with her when bidding her farewell
        how eerie her palm felt
Ever since your fetish for cleanliness has been so excessive
        that you cannot touch anybody else's body yet
Whenever you recall the male teacher's face
        the mower's face also leaps to your mind
Since the passive voice first trespassed on your knowledge
        you have not yet overcome your phobia of English

Parade

A woman picks up her underwear she cast off a while ago and puts it on again.

She turns to her man with a beautiful smile, and he sees her ugly warped nose again. Watching her naked body hidden slowly, he is assured: "Only when I'm with her, I can believe in the presence of mystery; without her, I cannot keep this courage to keep standing alone against this cruel world." After a glance at the self-absorbed face of her naked man, she starts telling him a story she told her every ex at least once:

"This is about the three girls I used to hang out with very often in my childhood. For convenience, I'll call them each Girl A, B and C. Girls A and B were looking forward to watching from the roadside an impending parade every adult was ardently calling either 'a once-in-a-lifetime pageant' or 'the greatest in this nation's history.' That would be their first and last chance to steal a quick look at the real face of the Heavenly Lord. The parents of Girl A always considered the Lord 'the origin of all the discrimination in this country' and secretly hated him so much. They didn't know their daughter secretly disdained them all the time. For her, the Lord was the one and only hero who would heal each wound in the minds of all his subjects. She stuck various kinds of the Lord's portrait on her diaries. She made it a midnight habit to stare at them alone and give soul kisses to his agonized faces, whispering: 'Our Lord's pain is for us.'

Girl B's father amassed great riches through his long career in mass-producing what captivated Girl A, that is, the Lord's portraits. His company was monopolizing this niche business. Girl B's mother, a Sunday painter, was always proud of her husband. Her paintings featuring the Lord were everywhere in her house. Girl B scorned her parents secretly, however. Repeatedly she said to herself: 'The Lord doesn't show his true emotions at all, but I can always guess them correctly. Now he's keeping to himself his revulsion against those who are making big money by abusing his divinity or making much ado without paying any due homage to him.'

Girl C had been alone all the time until she met Girls A and B. Utterly indifferent to everything about the Lord, she was putting the two friends of hers merely down as a pair of 'heavenliness maniacs.' She wanted neither to lose their friendship nor to return to her former heart-wringing solitude, so she always tried to follow their order: 'Love the Lord, otherwise we will punch you in the nose.' Whenever her lovely nose was distorted by their knuckles, Girls A and B looked all the more adorable to her.

On the very day of the parade, the three girls, putting on the same blood-colored dress and hand in hand, awaited on the crowded roadside the coming of the Lord's sublime vehicle. Catching a glimpse of his figure through the passing car window, Girl C was surprised; in her eyes, he looked simply feminine. Moreover, in her eyes, his gracious mouth seemed to whisper: 'You don't have to love me — whenever you love someone deeply, he or she will be your own true Lord.' Meanwhile, Girl B found herself driven by sexual desire while nailing the Lord's mysterious profile on her memory. She had never been so wildly titillated before. When Girl B was about to give her mind's ear to an unheard-of voice ('Love every mystery just as it is'), Girl A tugged the hands of the other two suddenly and burst from the crowd. The Lord's car was a stone's throw from them, and a weapon-like thing was in Girl A's hand. She yelled: 'Oh Lord, suffer more for the sake of our suffering!' Some security guards rushed to the three girls and hit them right in their faces. The lovely noses of Girls A and B were warped just like Girl C's and, seconds later, the bodies of the three started melting like a pulp — they blended with one another into some strange red liquid and dirtied the glorious road."

As soon as she finishes the story, the woman wipes out the blood from her groin, and covers her man's eyes entirely with a blindfold, as if to ridicule his innocent inquiry ("Who the hell is the Lord, anyway?"). She asks him if he is facing a "due confusion" he ought to face, and this unusual question turns him on. He pesters her for one more kiss, but she only says: "All you can get is a little peck on your unpatriotic nose, babe." Holding her blindfolded man affectionately in her arms, the woman wonders again: "Where can we discover the actual dividing line between patriotism and unpatriotism?"

A World Devoid of Dialogue

Why does such a wide variety of people gravitate to this square
All the way from the whole world over? Look how inconspicuous
This place is — there's nothing but an ordinary all-dry fountain
In its hub. Why does such a diversity of races and ethnic groups
Dare to visit here night and day? Among the big crowd is a poet
Who was born in this small town but hated its monotonousness
From his heart by his coming of age. He once left this birthplace
And was appreciated fully as a talented poet in a far country —
Now he has returned here after an interval of so many years to
Overcome a deep-rooted sense of fear that there may be neither
Material nor eagerness left to write new poems. He expects to be
Poetically inspired again by getting the uncanniness of this place
(The very center of his hometown) to rub off on him. As soon as
He joins the crowd floating here and there in the square, the poet
Realizes every one of them is merely thinking aloud — he or she
Is talking not to anyone else but to the void. An ostensibly merry
Young man standing next to the poet repeats to himself: "To hell
With the Coming-of-age Day!" This curse gradually shifts from
A whisper to a violent shriek, but nobody reacts to the young man.
A middle-age woman keeps mumbling to herself while lying alone
On the waterless bottom of the fountain: "Look, I'm an oyster —
Breeding me is the best way to reclaim contaminated water, but
The water here is too filthy for me alone to return to the enough
Clarity, despite your ardent wish to swim here again like before."
Meanwhile, all the gentlemen squatting in shabby suits around
The fountain are into the identical soliloquy while neglecting one
Another: "If you want to survive, you have to cultivate in yourself
A nerve to kill — lesson one for this cultivation is to murder your
Neighbors — when you dare to try it for the first time, you must
Not forget to laugh — enjoy!" So skeleton-like, their orderliness
Drives the poet into a strong feeling of nausea. Still, he walks on
And hears another monologue drifting from his right side: "We all
Had been too strictly taught not to doubt anything — and here is
The result." A different monologue creeps from his left: "We obey
Every command so blindly because we all don't know what love is."

Though they look like mutual lovers, two young people on a bench
Leak their respective monologues in the opposite direction from
The partner. One of them says: "When the earth cracks and the rift gulps
A majority of us, is privacy still needed for the fortunate survivors?"
The other says: "I've had enough of bipedalism — from now I will
Change into a salamander and sail alone in this sewer-like world
— I may often feel disgusted by too much muck and filth — but
I will eventually adjust well and start swimming composedly —
Even if a dead fetus happens to flow by." Worry strikes the poet:
"This absence of conversation may turn my poetry into nonsensically
Monological and second-rate" — as soon as he starts looking for
A companion, he sees the young Coming-of-age-day hater pointing
At the moonless sky and yelling: "Tonight smells like the moon!"
Unexpectedly, all the soliloquies in the square come to a halt.
The poet's imagination starts grinding slowly and shows him
A scene where each of the crowd mounts on the back of one another
To make a huge tower out of themselves. It also shows him a scene
Where a lonely wooden canoe sails across the ocean — no island is
Seen yet — "Is this the very inspiration I longed for?" — the poet
Feels this may be his final return to this small town — moreover
The entire crowd seems like a stained-glass window in his eyes.

The Start of the Cherry Blossom Season

The outcome of my latest physical checkup showed
The exceptional lack of magnet force in my body
I was swiftly carried to a hospital on a stretcher
The hospital's long name included my own name
A private sickroom on the basement was allotted
I lay on the bed and wondered when the doctors
Or nurses would come back again to my bedside
But nobody showed up — to escape the boredom
I left the sickroom — I stopped by the saloon and
Peeked from behind a pillar at what was going on
All the inpatients whiling away the afternoon there
In their respective fashion looked exactly like me
And placed in the center of the saloon was a rugged
Rock whose size and height were identical to mine
A caregiver-chief-like person appeared with a big
Smile and declared while caressing the surface of
The rock in a child-soothing way: "Folks — today
This friend of ours has recovered completely at last"
The announcement sounded dignified enough like
The Meteorological Agency proclaiming the start of
This year's cherry blossom season — one inpatient
After another started gravitating to the rock as if they
Were drawn to a magnet — the chief yelled stately:
"This fortunate one metamorphosed into this shape
While waiting for the return of its beloved who had
Left this hospital in the remote past — as you know
Nothing but this transformation testifies to complete
Recovery — regarding this state as death is a sin!"
One of the inpatients stroked the rock and mumbled:
"Every one of us should end this way sooner or later"
The others nodded in unison — one of them sighed:
"I wish I could be next" — another one questioned:
"What is the root cause of this awesome petrifaction?
Lament for the farewell? Fury over the betrayal of

Its lover?" — one pure speculation after another
Flew across the saloon: "Maybe this poor person's
Every emotion went numb during the eternal wait"
"No — this devil worried too much about public
Attention and ended up like this" — "Wrong —
This mate's love for the mankind came tumbling
Down — that is why!" The grinning chief threw
A fierce look at the ceiling as if to probe an enigma
Floating far and whispered: "No medically accurate
Answer is discovered yet" — the inpatients finally
Regarded their speculations as totally useless and
Followed the chief out of the saloon — I found
Myself willing to touch the rock — but — some
Invisible repulsive force stopped me from doing so
Then humanlike voice began escaping from the rock
"I was believing firmly and in vain that in this world
That person would be the only everlasting being like
God!" — scorn for the voice budded in the depth of
My atheistic mind as the rugged rock added: "I don't
Want to see myself with my own eyes — this is not
My body but somebody else's!" Then the rock's tone
Changed: "Ah — hiding right behind the pillar must
Be — finally returned?" The repulsion disappeared
And I rushed to the rock — my dry tongue began to
Lick all over its surface — the rock moaned: "More
Please — more!" — all the inpatients returned to
The saloon with their favorite musical instruments in
Their hands and started playing — a chorus began
Behind my back: "Ob-La-Di Ob-La-Da life goes on
Bra!" — my bloody tongue's slow lovemaking with
The rock went on — when can I leave this hospital?

Evacuation Order

"DANGER! DANGER! FLEE NOW! DO ALL YOU CAN TO PROTECT YOURSELF!"

Too many people are too easily driven into frenzy every time they encounter what doesn't make any sense to them — they cannot help snapping quickly: "Why must I understand this nonsense? Making it comprehensible enough is not my task!" — fearing as usual such a volatile world around you, you shut yourself up in your room again. You're still a little child. You try to slumber soundly, but in vain. As always, when you start having the dream of a big tree standing alone on the gloomy ground like the surface of Mars, the inevitable peremptory order resounds all over your town and wakes you up. Reluctantly,

"WHY ARE YOU STILL WANDERING ON THE PROVING GROUND? — SCRAM!"

you open the door, get out, and begin to run slowly on a midnight boulevard. "The proving ground? Enough fake news! This is my neighborhood, nothing but an ordinary residential area, and everything stays calm and quiet tonight." Nevertheless, you keep running just as you were ordered, because you're still a child. As if a ray of light is forcibly pulled out of the darkness, a tiny shelter looms up in front of you. You approach its door cautiously and tries to open it. But it is locked. You look through one of the windows and find several foreign women collapsing on the floor. Their worn-out faces remind you immediately

"DON'T TOUCH ANY LIVESTOCK CARCASS NEGLECTED HERE AND THERE!"

of the word "immigrants." The women turn to you at once and catch your eye. They say: "Even that boy will grow up to be as raunchy as other male beasts in his country; someday he will visit our country to buy some local women like us while looking down on them as if they were his livestock or something; he will return to his home as soon as he finishes getting laid with them. What a shame!" You have absolutely no idea what they're talking about, though, because you're still too young. Terrified by the women's intense stares, you begin to run again. After a while, when another shelter comes into your view, you feel as if the god

"SOMETIMES ZERO GRAVITY HITS YOU — BEWARE OF SUDDEN FLOATING!"

controlling chance took trouble to arrange it for the advent of your adulthood. Its door is also locked, though. You peep through one of the windows and see a girl sketching something alone, surrounded with library-like stacks of books. To your surprise, every book can speak like humans and seems to be in serious dispute with one another. One of the voices argues the best way to live happily is to surrender yourself completely to the fate granted by others. Another voice disagrees; it deems every contact with others pointless and asserts there will be no happy life without choosing how to die all on your own. Meanwhile, the girl

"DON'T TRUST ANYONE! TRUST ME ONLY, IF YOU WANT TO SURVIVE!"

keeps sketching with rapt attention. What she is drawing seems like some kind of animal, whose each body part shows an abstraction: its face has amazement; beauty is on the top of its head; doubt, hesitation, lust, and loneliness are lined vertically from its neck down to its chest; tangled up around its heart are unease, ease, hope and despair; on its right arm are sadness and suffering; hung from its left arm are pleasure and delight; its right leg is stuffed with hate, fear, and rage; its left leg is packed with love, pity, and mercy. The girl suddenly yells: "But for this ugly monster, I wouldn't have needed to evacuate!" She turns to the window

"REMEMBER: YOUR EVERY MOVE FROM SHELTER TO SHELTER IS TRACED!"

and catches your eye. Her astonishment seems as if she has come across her own corpse. Gradually, she is transformed into a sheep. Once her metamorphosis ends, she starts devouring every page of every book around her. As if you float through the air into different times, you move away from the shelter. Because you're still a child, you cannot notice the silent voices of your loved ones you left behind. I'll translate all their pure words literally for you: "You are a permanent deserter; you can never give up acting irresponsibly; whenever you move from one darkness to another, from one gender to another, just like an airy dancer, your footsteps will be

"FORGET ALL YOUR FAMILY AND FRIENDS YOU LEFT BEHIND!"

blown off by a gust of wind, just like grains of sand." Exhausted, you trudge up to a monumental tree standing alone. Its tapestry-like boughs and sprigs remind you of the sketch the girl was making until the start of her transformation. You

"DON'T DOZE ON THE ROAD LIKE THE HOMELESS DURING YOUR ESCAPE!"

lie down like an ox under the tree and begin to sleep. Again, however, the order of the same messenger reaches your ears from far as if to shake awake the dead.

Reli(e)ve

When my weary legs led me here at last
I felt as if I had been a reincarnation of Don Quixote
After trudging for days under the intense summer sunshine
To search for the whereabouts of my crush
Today I found myself on this seashore --- now my love interest is
Standing alone on the water's edge --- now is the time
To confess my whole hidden affection to that dear person

Lying under the love's feet is the carcass of a moray eel
Washed up dismally by the typhoon several days ago
Its eyes are completely hollowed out
Its skin looks like the imprint of the past storm

Jutting dismally from the moray's jawless mouth
Is the tail-side half body of a beautifully-tinted small tropical fish
Its resistance to the fierce swallow seems to have
Ended up sharing its ferocious predator's fate

My crush kicks lightly the moray's belly
And the moray's previous incarnation is projected
As a human male traveler all over the summer sky
Now the traveler is about to start off alone
For an uninhabited place dubbed "The Fallout City"

"Please don't look for me" --- leaving this short note
He departs at midnight silently from his home
He is determined to devote the rest of his life
To cleaning the ominous "F" city of all deadly ashes

There he will keep working without pay and holidays
He will share with his fellow workers a room in a ghetto
His cleaning tools will serve nothing but their chores
Ashes will keep accumulating in his lungs day after day
Every small change of his own condition will terrify him
He will often imagine no grave will be built for his death

"No one needs to tend my tomb" --- he will say to himself
While throwing a sidelong glance to his roommates sleeping
Next to him with a look of wrath against eternal hard work

Now the traveler smiles bitterly
His teeth are as white as the moray's fang

My love interest's kick relieves the tropical fish from the moray's mouth
Its face is awfully dissolved --- but its eyeballs still clearly show
The azure of the deep ocean --- coming gradually to their surfaces
Is the fish's previous incarnation --- a blind human woman in despair
Her husband plants one flower seedling after another
Around their house day after day only to comfort her
Years later --- their whole town changes into a big flower garden

Sometimes she nestles down into the flowers she cannot see
And sinks into the secret fantasy of being embraced by the waters

While looking down on the two fish carcasses
My dear person suddenly cringes --- is it caused by
The moray eel's desperate persistence in holding
The small prey in the face of its own imminent death?
Or by the tropical fish's misfortune to have shown
Itself to its evil predator on the day of the storm?
Or by the unfathomable blue of this cruel ocean
That simultaneously cleaned out the two creatures?

While walking slowly toward my crush from behind
(To embrace the cringing body and pledge my eternal protection)
Gradually appearing in my sight is a horde
Of dead human males and females lying
Around my dear person's feet like an illusion

Turning around and noticing my frightened face
My partner-to-be whispers vaguely only one word
Is it "relieve" or "relive"?
While jeering at my fleeting confusion
The waves gain momentum again and finally
Carry off the ugly bodies of the two fishes

Her Rainy Birthday

On your birthday you decide to meet no one and
Sit all alone at a plain table without anything on it
The sound of hard rain comes through the window
You wonder for the first time why you were born

Down on the square table's surface one faint line
After another appears vertically and horizontally
Now infinite infinitesimal squares are set before
Your eyes — in each of those squares you find

A pile of sand? — you focus a bit further — it is
A pile of fine-grained words like the sand of a dune
Each of those piles is preserved like an art treasure
In each minute square box and there appears to be

No vacant square on the table — "Oh not to worry
More new squares will be set soon" — you look up
And notice a middle-age gentleman with mustache
And glasses on sitting with a smile opposite you on

A chair that ought to be vacant — "All these words
Are the poems I dedicated to you in the past — once
I prepare another stack of words on why you are here
I'll come up with a new square box and keep it there"

What is this man chattering about? — who is he? —
You rest your chin on your hand and reach back in your
Mind — the distant memory of someone's affectionate
Hands massaging your body up and down recurs to you

The owner of the hands used to say: "You ought to live
A happier life — why do you fear happiness so often?"
Did you look at his face when you refused his "sermon"?
Did you notice any pair of spectacles or mustache there?

Now you open your eyes — you see only a pair of glasses
And a false mustache on the plain table — the opposite
Chair to you stays as vacant as before — all the vertical
And horizontal lines have already vanished — you trace

Their illusions with your finger — on your rainy birthday
You're listening to the sound of hard rain without meeting
Anyone — and you're waiting — until someone calling
Himself a "poet" appears and sits quietly right before you

Exorcism

It is your home country that occupied this foreign town for a long time.
The relics of a mansion standing in front of you used to be owned by
A family of one of the ruling colonizers. Now, the paint of its walls is
Scaling off. Its garden is almost like a dump. The past luxury of its gate
Has already disappeared and left some crumbling blocks. Look through
The cracks in its windows, and you will notice a bunch of wild animals
Having their own way on the ragged carpets or amid the dusty furniture.
After wondering for a while how alienated the two-story ruin's balcony
Looks from here and now, you shift your gaze to what is on your palm:
A black-and-white photograph featuring a pretty girl standing proudly
In this town's traditional dress with her eyes kept front. In the days of
Occupation, she was living in this mansion — on sunny mornings or
In cool evenings, probably, she showed herself on the balcony with her
Gently-smiling parents and looked down at the expanse of the colonial
Rule. Why was she able to live as a "legitimate child" in this mansion,
Although she apparently belonged to the occupied folk? — whereas
Toying with this mystery, you notice yourself facing a critical moment
Of decision, which may turn your way of life on its head. You grandly
Turn to the locals strolling down the street and declare loudly: "Please
Listen up, everybody — I decided to purchase this decrepit mansion
— I will renovate its entire structure and its garden, and make it alive
Again!" Unfortunately, though, none of the passersby can comprehend
Your foreign-language speech. They only give you a suspicious glance,
As if to say you are a pervert, and quickly pass you by. The exception
In this indifferent crowd is a matriarch-like old woman sitting down in
The shade of a tree while fastening her expressionless eyes on your face.
Obviously, you have never seen this woman before. In the knowledge
That she will never understand your speech, you elevate your voice to
Make yourself heard. You say your name first, and fluently talk about
Your home country, your personal belief, and your reasons for being in
This town and for having to buy this undone residence. The old woman
Reacts, again expressionlessly, to your foreign words by taking out from
Her chest a few pieces of beautifully-dyed cloth and waving them at you
Innocently, as if each one of them is her country's national flag. Somehow,
Their movement makes you imagine, with the sudden shivers, an aurora in

The northern sky. But it is only momentary, and, as soon as the aurora fades,
You begin to say to yourself confidently: "My purchase may seem impulsive
— But I'm not irresponsible at all — nobody but me is willing to make this
Bold decision — if this decision makes somebody else unhappy somewhere,
I'll happily assume full responsibility for it — as long as I fear such a risk,
I can never move forward!" Once you look at the photo again, two silhouettes
Loom up outside the frame of the creased black-and-white world. Probably,
One of them is the girl's father — look at his dignified manner and composed
Countenance — he talks to his daughter: "No matter how much the blood of
The inferior race is flowing in your body, I will keep protecting you with all
My force!" The other figure seems to be the girl's mother — she talks to her
Daughter: "Even in the inferior people there must be at least one great person,
My dear — and I know you are the one!" The more gently they speak to her,
The paler the girl looks and the more rigid her arms and legs seem. You cannot
Help intruding yourself into the bosom of this family. Despite the absence of
Their understanding of your native language, you start shouting your name,
Your home country, your personal belief, your reasons for being in this town
And for having to buy this undone residence. Every enunciated word of your
Fluent speech is quickly transformed, in the air, into a deadly sharp weapon,
Disregarding your cheerful face. One of the weapons gouges out the eyes of
The mother. Another of them cracks her brain. The father's neck is slashed
Horizontally. His chest is stabbed repeatedly, his belly slit up deeply, and his
Penis mutilated at last. Blood is all over the floor of the mansion — once its
Task is finished, each weapon scatters everywhere in the residence and starts
Repairing each horrible sight in this immense wreckage. All the walls recover
Their previous beauty. The garden regains its old refinement. The main gate
Recaptures its past stateliness. All the wild animals are completely expelled.
The glory of a bygone age starts illuminating every piece of furniture again.
A stillborn baby falls out of the chasm of the father's beefy abdomen (Is this
The vestige of his desire to put himself into a woman's pain?). The mother's
Thoroughly-skinned face reveals distinctly its longtime secret: the features of
The local people in this town (Is this the remnant of her desire to put herself
Into the colonized?) "I'm always responsible for my every word and deed!"
— Your explanation of your own personal background and philosophy seems
Unstoppable. When floods of your knife-like words are about to strafe the girl,
An aurora emerges in the sky and starts falling down on you. Something like
An indescribably soft cloth mask covers your entire mouth. Someone's hand
Appears from behind you and holds the gag gently. Into your ear, someone's

Silky whisper starts flowing (It's this town's local language) — isn't it saying
This way?: "It is almost time for you to take a rest — first, sit with me under
That tree" — or this way?: "I used to be the very girl on the photo you have."
Your innermost begins to reconstruct itself as if it is guided by the aurora. How
Much will the trace of your own past remain intact after the repair? Who will
Generously purchase you as his or her residence? Now, tears are in your eyes.

Water Thief

Feeling everything unbearably disgusting,
You ran and ran from all things about you.
Now you're standing on a spectacular dam
Located among mountains. Looking down
On the immensity full to the brim with black
Water, you feel so hungry and wonder why
There is not a shadow of houses around you.
Out of the blue, a loudspeaker starts to repeat
The explanation about the history of a village
Submerged due to the completion of the dam.
Until the day of its disappearance, the village
Had been supplied neither with water nor with
Electricity — each of a few remaining villagers
Used to wake up before every dawn, shoulder
A long wooden pole with two worn-out pails
At its either end, and walk over several steep
Mountains every morning to a faraway town
Where they could finally get drinkable water.
It was their community's daily routine dating
Back several hundred years, and shortly after
The town's only communal well upon which
The villagers had long depended was closed,
They started knocking on the door of every
Towner's detached house or apartment house.
Like beggars, they bowed down and solicited
A glassful of water without embarrassment.
By the time they walked back to their village,
Their pails were so heavy with the collected
Water — the slightly bent poles wedged into
Their exhausted shoulders and had them walk,
Every evening, silently with dragging feet —
While you hear the speaker's repeated words
With your dull eye on the dam's black water,
The water surface changes into a silver screen
As if to show a brand-new movie only to you

And an unfamiliar woman shows up on it —
She used to be one of the villagers, but now she
Lives, after the forced eviction, in a town where
Your house is located. Nobody is in your house
Due to your absence — with her pails-attached
Pole on her shoulders, she trespasses quietly on
Your garden — and steals water, till both of her
Pails are full, from the tap furnished in its corner.
Doesn't she know the water in her pails is from
What brought her village to ruin? She begins to
Drag herself to her current place while enduring
The murderous weight of two pailfuls of water.
Now she lives on the uppermost floor of the most
Splendid skyscraper in the town. Why does she
Ignore the elevators in the building and choose to
Walk up the emergency stairs like a lonely slug?
Her shoulders are almost squashed — her body
Is already covered in sweat — she has long kept
Imposing this agony on herself day after day since
She moved here. And your house's tap has been
The easiest target in this town for her. Her floor
Is completely unlike all the downstairs ones
Where luxurious residences are lined in order.
It is merely a plain rooftop where all you can see
Is her miserable hut and a small patch of greens
On the slabs of concrete. How did she convey
This soil up there all on her own? From where?
Quietly, she begins to pour the water in the pails
On her poorly growing vegetables. No water, no
Electricity, no gas is automatically supplied here
In this solitary rooftop life, whereas everything is
Plenty down below. Some memories start flowing
Through her mind as she gulps the leftover water
In the pails: the violence of her late husband who
Forced her to live with him here against her will;
The night she sobbed with grief right after her
Failed escape from him; the face of her dead son
Who was brought up on the rooftop since his birth.

Suddenly — fireworks color the sheer darkness
Beyond the dam and surprise you. Without notice,
An unknown man stands right near you and says:
"Did you also choose this place as your life's final
Destination? I'm very glad to have a mate like you.
This dam is like a giant toilet where you can flush
Anything, don't you think?" You wonder whether
The woman is watching the same fireworks alone
On the rooftop or not. Also, you start missing home.

Loquat Tree

Humping
the dead body
of your beloved
who desired her own remains

Not to be buried but to be exposed to the elements, you're now trudging
Alone in the woods --- you know what you're doing is illegal in this country
Your destination is the place she secretly told nobody but you
About in her lifetime --- the venue she chose for her final journey

The very moment her soul was gone, you forbade yourself to watch
The subsequent change of her body --- since then, you have kept closing
Your eyes tight --- now you're walking like a blind man, putting up with
The heavy weight of reality, toward her open resting place --- the valley

Of great antiquity where she used to wander alone --- your unseeing eyes
Are still glued to the memory of your beloved's naked body in the last
Stage of medical treatment --- in those days, even when the levels of her
Tumor markers were extremely high, she insisted: "Now I'm heading for

A new life, not death --- the marker levels have risen because detoxification
In my system is running smoothly!" --- she dismissed every advice to have
An operation ("No more science!" was her pet phrase) and persisted in her
Self-taught therapy until her last --- she plucked hundreds of loquat leaves

And put every one of them not only on the diseased part but also on other
Important regions of her undressed body --- she placed moxa on each of them and
Burned it --- she trusted this method, and the only loquat tree she relied on
Is standing in the valley you're travelling to --- "That tree will never betray

Me," she always said --- she endeavored to write a will with her shaky hand
But her every attempt never reached what she had expected --- her final draft
Had only one sentence: "Dump me in the valley" --- then another voice from the bush:

"If she could have precisely imagined the shape of death, her will would have been
Far more solid" --- with her on your back, you turn around and ask: "Who is it?" ---
"Are you blind? Let's face it --- Homer, Milton, and other renowned poets in history are
All blind --- how will you treat the heavy thing on your back, anyway?"

The voice speaks again to your firmly closed eyes: "Unless I'm mistaken
Aren't you heading for the valley? Let me tell you something, then --- it is
Me who owns the valley, which is, in fact, a big mine of natural uranium
Everything has betrayed me, except uranium!" --- the dead weighs on you

More heavily --- you reach the bottom of the valley and confront at last
The loquat tree for the first time --- expanding around you is a broad trace
Of the wildflowers your beloved kept plucking, while believing blindly that
Eating them raw would eventually help heal her --- you deposit the dead gently

On the ground --- her bare vagina seems to hover between obscene reality
And beautiful abstraction --- "Adieu," you whisper, and feel sudden fear
Because the mummified face seems to have replied: "Now this disease is
In your system, too --- you will become an orphan like me, sooner or later"

You finally open your eyes when you leave her and return --- you have
No idea where you are in the lightless woods --- after meandering, you will
Notice a hint of human presence --- you peer into the dark to find various
Minerals covering someone's body as fungi do --- you ask: "Who are you?"

The reply sounds familiar: "You again? Since my birth I've been too tired
To move --- I cannot even open my mouth enough --- but I have hidden
This woeful truth perfectly until now --- haven't you, also? --- that's why
Your body is all covered with those leaves --- am I wrong, young man?"

Feeling more fear, you turn around again to look for the right return road
Your eyes are fixed on the distant light of a power plant --- its life-giving
Flicker may make death deader --- you feel relieved and restart walking
Silently, imagining what the future would be like for all dropouts from death

Love Triangle

While almost dying on the hospital bed slowly
tranced by general anesthesia, this inpatient
babbled again as always: "Fate selected me as
the only immortal person in this whole world
without regard to my serious itch to be mortal"

Was the moribund patient a woman in male attire
or a man in female attire? — the one and only
caregiver in this sickroom was an old man sitting
right at the bedside — his oddly wrinkled face
showed neither compassion nor sympathy — so

blank in my eyes peeking from this secret shade
Nobody knew correctly about the relations among
the patient and the caregiver and me — for long
I had adored and worshipped the moribund —
I had offered everything I had to the dying —

the old man deprived me of the right to caregiving
and schemed to keep the patient's ending to himself
Why did that self-centered fellow resemble me in
appearance so much? — shown on the front page
of the paper in his hand were my particulars like

height / body shape / hair / clothes / shoes and so on
There I was labelled the missing — the dying's body
was in the throes again — the caregiver's mind was
icy enough after all his daily efforts for the consolation
of the patient's soul — he had every reason to feel so

The patient tyrannically blamed the loyal attendant's
incompetence for all the anguish welling up on bed
"Do you really believe a miracle will take place and
my pain will immediately go away? Stop spending
day and night kneeling in such unwise prayer and

bring me a more decent doctor as soon as you can!
Bring here a more powerful medicine right away!"
The caregiver started calculating again the budget
and the scenario of the impending funeral service
whereas the hoarse voice rose afresh from the bed

"I envy your breathing and walking and eating and
speaking normally — watching your every move
worsens my condition" — the caregiver wondered
again quietly when the much-wanted death would be
coming to this room — the hoarse voice continued

"Why must I live permanently in spite of this limitless
pain? — why must I survive alone while all the others
in the world will be destined to perish? — why must I
create alone the new mankind?" — ah — I remember
the patient saying to me long ago — "Lick my blood

and you will turn immortal" — "Now must be the time
to replace this caregiver" — this self-energizing voice
sounded so beautiful while my face in the mirror seemed
ugly enough due to jealousy — with a dagger I stabbed
the old fellow in the back — the unexpected visit of death

and my abrupt entry terrified the caregiver — "You will
know someday the utmost importance of giving up things
You will even give up breathing while in lifetime custody
here" — his last word — the corpse on the floor made
me realize the terror of shame and guilt for the first time

I covered my devastated face with my hands — a hand
reached feebly and started uncovering my face gently —
the smiling moribund's one — my life thereafter kept
unfolding only within this sickroom under a vow of dying
a martyr following the inpatient's latter end — however

the moribund remained moribund — "Heaven and pure
land are not in the sky but on the earth — the shapes of
both of them are nothing but vacant" — the inpatient's
favorite phrase — the dying slowly began to be relieved
from the agony through my devout nursing care — more

and more peaceful smiles — my soul leaned totally upon
the moribund whose body leaned solely on me till that day
It was the patient's casual question that made our intimacy
go wrong — "You took a huge risk in reaching this place
A number of people must be still making tremendous efforts

to search for you — don't you need their support at all?"
I said "No" — to my surprise — the moribund started
cursing me — "What? Do you think you can do anything
only at your own risk? Liar! Your words are nothing but
vacancy!" — the dying's first stream of abuse against me

The patient's hands totally covered the moribund face —
my hands managed to uncover it gently when I could not
help asking myself a tough question: "Perhaps — isn't
the next missing right behind my back? Isn't she peeking
from the shade with a dagger in her hand as I once did?"

Tunnel

Ah those days — I was always weeping up to exhaustion
Owing to the absence of mutual understanding and trust
The only relief came from an ordinary middle-age fellow
Living alone right at the back of my house — I had not
Exchanged any greetings with him till then — standing
In his old garden was an ancient-looking cherry tree with
Its every branch fantastically formed — it had never had
Any bloom if my memory is correct — an old noose was
Tied firmly to the most robust-looking branch — roughly
Two meters high — I still vividly remember the first time
I talked with him in person — somehow he was going to
Hang himself with the noose — He noticed me rushing to
Stop him and said: "No worries — this is just my hobby"
The rope began to squeeze his neck — the gradual spread
Of lethargy over his arms and legs — the ghastly moves
Of his eyeballs — more and more foam around his mouth
Shivers ran silently through me — after a several-minute
Horrifying writhing he finally got his neck out of the noose
And thumped down on the ground — and he told me that
Around every midnight he regularly did this weird imitation
I said: "You were just like the dead!" — he shyly returned
To his house without any reply — since then we were on
Speaking-sometimes-under-the-tree-around-midnight terms
I kept asking: "Why did you decide to make it your habit?"
His answer was volatile — sometimes he said: "I can meet
My younger self thanks to gravity" — or "My teenage self
Used to keep wondering about his future while looking up at
This tree — I must give him the information on his inevitable
Future events" — his realistic performance went on and on
Without any pause — whenever I asked him half-jokingly
What he specifically explained to his younger self — with
All his teeth lost and all his hair white for his age owing to
Hanging himself too many times — he turned to me and

Whispered with the liveliest look I had never seen: "This
Is what I said to him tonight: someday your mind will be
Put forcibly between two different voices and suffer —
One will command you to live differently from others and
The other will order you to follow others — however —
He merely showed me a blank look" — or — sometimes
He said: "This is what I will say to my younger self tonight:
Someday you'll meet the one and only woman you'll love
Till your final day — she'll be terribly afraid of something
But won't show what it is all about — you will take her to
A variety of art exhibitions because looking at paintings is
Her only hobby — the last exhibition you'll enjoy with her
Is about Hieronymus Bosch — while staring at innumerable
Weird personas flooding on his every paradise and hell —
She'll mutter: 'I want this kind of place' — then you will
Have to reply: 'I'll be such a space for you' — you must"
My hanging-loving friend added that the woman had died
Long ago — I asked him about the cause of her death —
He asked me to ask no more — and slowly — started
Hanging himself again — he continued performing death
Every single midnight thereafter to have his younger self
Say what he had missed saying at that moment in spite
Of himself — during his absence the ring of the noose
Looked like a tunnel barely bridging hazy yesterdays and
Distant tomorrows — my friendship with this neighbor
Ended when I moved out to my current place — my last
Word to him during his live hanging act: "I understand" —
His reply: "Thank you very much for such a beautiful lie"
Right after the successful act he looked so fresh and alive

When can I meet
The one and only
I will keep loving
Until my very last
Will I also look at
An opus of Bosch
Together with her

If yes — we may discover in some corners of his masterpiece
A lonely man hanging himself or a naked man in ecstasy over
Being choked off by his lover during their sexual intercourse —
In my last garden in my life — will I find my dearest standing
Alone — or will I find a single old cherry tree standing alone
If the latter is the case — can I notice any blossom on the tree

At a Department Store

Even in this town, the national memorial service appears to be held
On a large scale. Meanwhile, you are still impatiently waiting for
A down elevator to rush to your lover waiting for you on the first
Floor. Waiting for the same elevator behind you is a group of men
Wearing the identical T-shirt whose chest says: "Wondering If We
Are LGBTQ? Yes, We Are! So What?" When you cast a glance at
This sentence, the next elevator comes at last. You get into it, and
It is your careless mistake. This is an up one, nonstop until the top
Floor. To make matters worse, it is already congested and no more
Space seems to be left once you thrust into it. Helplessly, you close
Your eyes and hold your breath. Your face is less than an inch away
From the elevator door. You strive to recall how your lover behaved
On your last date. A hoarse voice like an old woman's rises up from
Your back (apparently from beside the opposite wall) and penetrates
The silence of the closed crowd: "Look there — so many doves are
Flying, everybody — the memorial service seems to have started."
The door of the elevator is made only of transparent glass, and so is
The opposite wall. Thus you can see every department floor passing
At dazzling speed, whereas you can fully enjoy the panoramic view
Of the town if you stand right before the opposite wall. The moment
The bustle of the shoe department speeds away in front of your eyes,
The hoarse voice starts mumbling melodiously: "Everything was hell
Right after the war — that day — my kid and I were in a crowded
Train — it was simply as crowded as this elevator — my daughter
And I were crouching miserably near the door — my husband? —
He was a soldier at the front and there was no indication of his return
Yet — poverty was almost unbearable then and I was always asking
My hubby in my mind whether it would be high time for his wife and
Only kid to kill themselves — the train was shabby and its door was
Dangerously loose — pushing my little kid off the running train was
Like a cinch — she was drawing a picture of a pair of small shoes on
An old flier she had picked somewhere else — the shoes seemed like
The ones her dad had bought her — she was using a pencil stub with
Rapt attention." This monologue somehow reminds you of your lover
Telling you the other day about the outline of her favorite classic short

Story: "A man kills his wife and cat with an ax; he buries their corpses
In a wall; the dead cat's voice escapes from the wall; the man's crime
Is finally revealed; he is executed in the end." The elevator now passes
The bedclothes department, and the old woman's voice still continues:
"The other day my husband appeared suddenly in my mother-in-law's
Dream; she heard the quiet footsteps of military boots and a knock on
Our house door; without knowing it as a part of the dream, she opened
The door and saw her son standing downcast with his military uniform
Thoroughly soaked; 'Welcome home, son,' she said, trying to embrace
Him; he replied: 'I could have survived if I had had courage to degrade
Myself, Mother — I'm sorry.' That was the end of her dream. I don't
Understand why he hasn't showed up in my dream yet. What a shame."
You find all the other people in the elevator seem to hail from overseas.
You ask yourself: "Wasn't this country of mine a damnable foe of theirs
In the remote past?" The showy nail-salon floor flashes forth. "Yes — I
Received from the government an official report of my husband's death
In war — who in the world believes in what the government says? —
Since then I have been utterly poor with this child — I began to work
In a tiny factory for the first time in my life — my fingers were caught
In the cogwheels there and — " You barely turn your face to the opposite
Wall to see two wrinkled hands raised feebly over the heads. No fingers.
"The factory owner compelled me to be his woman — he was married
And had some children — I tried to refuse it, of course, but he said my
Pay would rise, so — I said okay in tears — his wife found his affair
Later and called me 'Thief Cat' — 'I want to beat both of you to death
With an ax,' she said." The elevator reaches the top floor at last and you
Get out with all the others in which you cannot find any old woman. As
The elevator door starts to close, a dove swoops down from the blue sky
And collides with the opposite wall. Somebody says to the bloodsoaked
Glass: "Did you come see me all the way? How merciful!" This voice and
The bird are slowly concealed from you as if they are buried in a wall.
The last words of the voice: "You all have the freedom to get out, while
I'm enjoying the freedom not to do so." In front of the elevator you see
A group of women wearing the very same LGBTQ T-shirt that you came
Across on the down floor. Their each back demonstrates the same words:
"You Straight People Also Have Some Serious Secret to Reveal, Right?"
Some of the women look at you and whisper to one another: "That guy is
Taking the elevator time and again and going up and down, up and down
— How creepy!" You start waiting for a down elevator to come and open.

Commuters

I know your secret --- you're now living only with an old poet
While the poet is about to finish his regular morning task, that is,
writing with rapt attention his new poem, you say "See you later"
merrily to the artist's hunched back and spread your flashy wings

Once you close the door and start commuting to your workplace
you change from a human being to a parrot --- you always walk
to work (without flying in the sky) from your residence, which is
located at the east end of a straight street lined with new houses

Until yesterday the color of your plumage was snow white, but
this morning it is somehow pure gold --- meanwhile, your crown
is as showy as ever --- today, as always, you must show your body
in your zoo cage and entertain every visitor until the closing time

Appearing from a house located at the west end of the same street
is a locally famous centenarian --- with an old hoe on his shoulder
he always calls himself a "farmhand for this street only," although
no soil to plow exists in this area, all of which is totally concreted

Here is this farmhand's favorite soliloquy: "Ho-ho, everyone says
this world is quite hard to live in, but --- he-he, believe me or not,
some folks are saved only because this world remains just as it is
Sometimes we have to hark to their 'saved' voices, too --- ha-ha!"

You keep walking at a smart pace to the west, while the hoer plods
to the east on the same sidewalk --- you mimic the aged poet's pet
phrases --- it sounds like a litany spilling from a mind depending on
someone else's gentle care --- your trick sounds as easy as a hum:

"A poem without proper temperament is mere garbage" --- *"Reality kills
a poem"* --- *"Objectivity always ruins poetry"* --- *"Poetry demands a gift
for dreaming of the unseen"* --- *"No sense-making! No intellect! And no
more science!"* --- meanwhile, the farmhand begins his everyday task

He knocks each new house's door while casting an eye over its front
yard paved with asphalt and speaks through the intercom: "Howdy!
Your soil looks best for plowing --- you must be too occupied to tend it
by yourself, so I will plow it in your place for free" --- as usual, no one

responds to his gentle voice --- his rotten hoe repeats a blunt metallic
sound right at his feet --- a long time ago --- when an infant was nearly
drowned in a deep ditch near the street, he plunged into the blackness
and saved her, disregarding all the crowd getting wet feet behind him

A long time ago --- he saw an infant fiddling alone innocently with
a soiled piece of paper money on the sidewalk and preached to her:
"Death by bacterial infection through dirty paper money is hell; so is
death by poverty due to dumping such dirty bank notes" --- when

you pass him on the street, your shiny beak does not give up imitating
what the poet whispers occasionally to himself: *"Nothing in this whole
universe is untranslatable"*--- *"The absolute truth, the absolute good,
and the absolute beauty are available all the time"*--- *"No gods have any*

*substance, and you should put your full faith in poetry rather than in such
stupid illusions! Poetry's every fixed pattern is a true religion!"* --- but ---
all the words and expressions in his new poem, the one he has finished
writing now, are in complete antithesis to the words you are mimicking

When the poet is about to take breath after the hard task, his intercom
conveys the farmhand's soothing voice: "Good morning, sir --- are you
writing a poem now? --- I remember you said you can change anything
into a poem --- but I'm afraid there are still plenty of things your poetic

capacity can hardly deal with --- I've heard that your poetry always ends
grotesquely --- why is a happy ending so despicable for you? --- and ---
shall I plow your garden soil for nothing, sir?" --- incidentally --- I know
this centenarian's top secret --- the most important thing for him through

his entire life is his old hoe, which barely survived that long war together
with him --- by the time the farmhand ends his daily morning round and
returns home, your crown embedded with a great deal of rays of the sun
is the center of attention in the zoo as usual --- have a good day, my friend

Somewhere in This Country

Somebody knocks at my window in the middle of the night
to warn me that a big fire broke out in my neighbor's house
"Wake up," the warner screams — I'm not falling asleep yet

I find myself lying next to a complete stranger lying awake
The stranger asks me a sudden question: "Listen — what
do you think you will wish for earnestly on your deathbed?"

The warner yells: "The fire is almost catching your house!"
Another outside voice mingles with it: "The justice is ours!
War is not our option but theirs! — now no other choice!"

Fire? That's a flat lie — tonight is as ordinary as last night
But my eyes notice smoke creeping into this room — am I
sleeping and dreaming? — this smoke is nothing but real

What will I wish for when I die? — smoke divides into two
One is black, which metamorphoses into a wiry male flesh
The other is white, which becomes a bewitching female body

The male's machoism and the female's eroticism work me up
Green with envy, I grab, before I know it, my old camera and
approach the two naked bodies — the lying stranger smiles

bitterly and says: "You have not slept a wink for a long time
That's exactly the reason you cannot imagine why my entire
body keeps convulsing madly like this" — from the outside

another voice rises: "Let's band together to put out this fire!"
I'm not the type who is easily deceived by such a cheap lie
But I must admit I'm slowly falling into this clever deception

My eyes are intoxicated by the male's beautiful muscles and
led simultaneously to the most intimate section of the female
though I know both of them are mere smoke — the stranger

adds while drooling perpetually: "I cannot see, I cannot walk
I cannot sit, and I cannot stand up at all" —I have never seen
such a lovely smile before — I look through the viewfinder to

take photos of the man and the woman — I see their nudities
entirely covered by a cloud of flies — whether my old camera
has captured their realities clearly or not becomes my big bother

An apology is repeated outside — it sounds offensively polite
"We'll promise to pay you an indemnity on condition you cease
to accuse us of our past faults" — creeping and nestling up

to me is the stranger's twisted-string-like torso: "Look at this
all-deprived body of mine — believe me or not, you and I used
to be one!" — meanwhile, I wonder what objects used to be

shot by this camera before I owned it — smoke keeps intruding
on me — the two naked figures disappear and a different scene
appears — in this new landscape, my children are glaring at me

The air is difficult to inhale without hesitation — the universe
cracks — honey starts to ooze from every part of the stranger's
body — the slobbering paralyzed mouth opens again: "Still now

a good number of people are tricked by this secretion into dreaming
about living close to me" — all my children pose a question to me:
"Was that an accident? Is our pain the result of heredity? If so —

how will you account for it?" How shall I respond to this complaint?
The warner bangs the window again and again — "Hey, wake up!
The fire is right here!" Meanwhile, another voice declares brightly:

"Now is the time for our reconciliation ceremony!" — I can see
behind my children a long straight road stretching to the horizon
and an endless procession of unknown children frozen on the road

"Do you still believe love is the only reason behind each creature's child raising? Bah! That's a stupid illusion!" — the honey-covered face says so, while gazing at every stage of my own metamorphosis

The rhythm of hula vibrates the window — it implies the liveliness of the reconciliation ceremony — someone's cry: "Nothing can halt science!" — both the rhythm and the cry must be only for tourism

Will I drown myself in sleep as if, say, a fly is drowned in honey? "Look at yourself — now you're a turtle — you're hibernating in the shell," the stranger says, while enduring bouts of convulsions

All the children on the road are still motionless — "Why have they inherited my name against their wishes?" — the turtle wonders in the shell whether it should stretch its grotesque neck to look outside

One-minute Outing

When did I start working as launderer?
My memory doesn't go that far anymore
I wonder why I'm still washing dirty clothes
of strangers day and night
Again I give a cruel boot to this old washing machine
(the only tool of my trade) as if I abused my longtime mate
I yell: "If I'm a loser, you are much worse!"

It is time to offer the routine silent prayer
Who must we all perform this futile ritual for everyday?
Which afterworld can be soothed entirely
by our eyes closed all at once for no more than a minute?
Today's foamy laundry starts rolling with a groan
in the machine — this moment seems to be the only
testament to the world's full recognition of me

I close my eyes reluctantly and see a taxi
dashing out of the darkness to pick me up
"Where to?" — my destination fails me
The taxi pulls off slowly
while its inside smells slightly rotten
Along every street a row of houses appears to be empty
The first ten seconds have passed

The driver finds out that I'm not a local
and starts explaining the history of the town:
"Here we used to have a language of our own
but the government banned us from learning it
Now only few of us can use it for reading and writing"
The taxi pulls up and another passenger
with a moai-looking face gets on and sits next to me

The next ten seconds have passed with a raw fish's smell
The driver starts explaining again:
"It is utterly shameful for me to have to live

without knowing our ancestral language
which has disappeared like a mirage"
My fellow passenger says quietly: "I'm fluent in it"
A thick mist begins to cover the whole town

Every shape in the town melts slowly
Another ten seconds have passed
Another moai-looking passenger gets on
The smell in the car turns more beastly
The driver starts explaining about himself:
"I used to be a soldier in the ongoing war
I killed some enemies and got interned

in the middle of the uninhabited plain
and returned here for my life recently"
The ongoing war? Which war is he talking about?
Another ten seconds have passed
The other two passengers begin their conversation
in a language totally unknown to me
The driver says: "The most meaningless thing in the world

is often the most meaningful for us — am I wrong?"
The taxi pulls up again and another moai-looking passenger
gets on (with a high-priced-looking tuning fork in hand)
The smell in the car turns grassy this time
Another ten seconds have passed
Ten more seconds to go until the end of the prayer
The latest passenger introduces himself as conductor

and asks the driver to go to the biggest concert hall in town
I ask: "What kind of music will you play there?"
"The number my orchestra plays tonight has a story —
it is about a human being who must live with injuries all over
while humping all the sins of mankind — its hardest part
for me to conduct is its every caesura"
The tuning fork rings and echoes gracefully

The taxi stops and the prayer ends
I open my eyes and the washing machine

has already finished all its tasks
Every laundry I take out of it still smells
fishy or beastly or grassy
I cannot help giving another fierce kick to the machine
which is already injured all over — I yell:

"Isn't washing clothes your only reason for being?
No gain without pain like this! Like this! Like this!"

Drifting out of the bottom of the machine is
a faint smell of newborns

Sacred Beast

"Bye for now, Mother" --- the woman leaves the room quietly
and goes out of the building --- under the fine summer sky she
turns around and looks up --- she discovers her mother gazing
far away, leaning against her balcony's fence --- the mother's
routine has just started again --- she always slips out of her bed

after her only daughter disappears from her bare private room ---
the woman has an urge to shout to her mother and ask ("What
can you see up there?"), but suppresses it quickly --- she knows
her old mother can listen to nothing but her own voice --- as if

to trace someone over an unfolded map, the mother moves her
finger before her own face and yells: "Ah, locusts are coming!"
The daughter still remembers the astonishment she faced when
she finally noticed her mother was developing a rare symptom:

in the mother's eyes, every convenience good is always seen as
her beloved human being --- whenever, in her favorite shopping
mall, she happens to find some packs of sanitary napkins sold
like filth under a shelf for men's weekly magazines, she says to

her daughter: "Ah, here is your father --- or --- mine?" (they are
already dead, though) --- "Try not to correct her deed by force,"
the daughter was once told, "otherwise some other issues would
surely show" --- as she looks up again, her mother's monologue

is gathering vigor: "What a large army --- today may be my last
day for plowing the field on fine days and reading books on wet
days on this desert island!" --- the mother used to have the habit
of saying: "I prefer a life full of 'maybes' to that inundated with

'definitelies'" --- no sooner does the daughter start recollecting it
than her mother points a finger to her from the balcony and yells:
"Look down there, people, it's a renowned plague-beating sacred
beast!" --- "By for now" --- when the daughter whispered so and

was about to walk out of the mother's single room a few days ago,
a baffling remark abruptly spilled from the inpatient's old mouth
The daughter still remembers it: "People say multiplication and
addition are two sides of the same coin, but --- tomorrow morning,

I want to stroll alone in a place where the two are totally separate
from each other" --- the mother shouts from the balcony: "Nobody
can kill our sacred creature!" --- she sees the army of locusts shade
into a ferocious pack of hounds --- a man levelling a shotgun at her

behind the dogs seems to be indifferent to the definition of "normal"
The daughter remembers both her father and grandfather used to say
to her during their lifetime: "The zest of living always lies in finding
a missing link among things totally unrelated to one another" --- she

even remembers her mother standing quietly behind the two men with
a sneer --- "Do you even sneer at me?" --- as the daughter mumbles so
the old mother is still captivated by the holy brute's gallant posture ---
its massive horns, its muscular muscles, its eyes full of enlightenment

and its unmoved spirit gazing at the muzzle aiming at its own forehead
"It's time for you to fly like a feather, hear me? --- take off with your
wild nature and bravery utterly intact!" --- the mother shouts so in her
heart while drooling like a dog --- her saliva falls onto the daughter's

cheek --- the hand wiping it off looks exactly like that of a matriarch
spreading her own blood all over her heir's baby face --- "By for now,
Mother" --- when the daughter walked out of the upstairs room slowly
and looked up at the balcony from the street, she saw the mother in a

blood-red costume standing all alone and snapping her fingers like
a rock star --- "Who the hell can wear this ugly thing?" --- the mother
roared, kicked her red high heels away, and, tearing her beautiful hair
and swinging her small body from side to side, started singing a song

in a voice unfamiliar to the daughter: "WHEN THE TIME COMES /
I WILL LEAP THOSE FARAWAY CLOUDS / WHEN THE NIGHT
COMES / I WILL SHOW YOU THE BEST MUSIC" --- "You don't
have to do anything special for your mother --- just stay close to her"

Keeping the medical advice in mind, the daughter tries searching for
the high heels on the street --- she meets a pet dog tied to a post with
a twisted cord --- smiling at it running around the post, she whispers:
"Why running so for nothing, doggie? The cord will be more twisted

and more shortened --- you will be utterly stuck to the post in the end"
Approaching the dog to loosen the twist, the daughter feels the animal
looking exactly like herself --- she turns around and looks up again ---
her mother is still standing alone over there, looking into the distance

Drain

My only remembrance of the day you were born is
    the illusion of an empty coffin which loomed
        from behind a shroud of darkness veiling the back of my pupils
            when I was pushing you out against pains
                with my eyes tightly closed

"Why don't you pretend to be the dead and lie there?" —
    wasn't that you who inspired me innocently then?
        As soon as I stretched out inside the coffin
            the lid was shut right in my face
                The darkness got far darker

when I saw you and called to your decrepit back:
    "Where are you going alone?" — you answered:
        "I'll go there and drain the whole water away"
            We walked through a dense forest and found a field where
                heaps of wastes were illegally dumped in rows

You called the whole field "the Pond"
    But no water could be seen anywhere — you said:
        "This place will surely go back to normal
            once we drain this coal-like muddy water
                and clean its bottom thoroughly together"

You started looking for the stopper of the Pond
    But there was nothing like that at all
        You began to explain kindly the history of the Pond
            during your strenuous search — long time ago
                its entire bottom used to be a dry depression

Two different tribes lived there — they were neighbors
    but despised each other — one of them was
        merely narcissistic and nostalgic — the other was
            partial to self-help and liberty
                and anarchistic — their mutual hatred peaked

They assaulted each other — both of them were
    victims and victimizers — it was right after that
        when the black water started to flow
            into the hollow ground and
                changed the vast expanse into the Pond

Some survivors of the two tribes pardoned
    each other in the water — they even became friends
        Was that really their spontaneous decision?
            Was there really no mental conflict in each of them?
                According to the explanation escaping from your aged mouth:

"Two dry sheets of glass can never stick to each other
    But they can with the mere help of one drop of water
        on their surfaces — so can the two darks of human mind"
            The survivors transformed themselves into fishes under water
                Some became local breeds and the others non-native species

They are said to have coexisted
    peacefully ever after —
        is that really how such a story is supposed to end?
            Isn't an ecosystem of natives usually ruined by aliens?
                First of all — where are those heaps of wastes from?

Who in the world left them here?
    Why are they left intact still now?
        You called this place "the Pond" — but
            others may put different names to it
                I may be the only person who can see the heaps now —

You were still looking for the absent stopper
    Suppose you found it and pulled it out
        what would you discover on the bottom?
            Babies discarded by their parents and drowned?
                Senile parents discarded by their grown-up kids?

Or — the extraordinary confusing the ordinary?
    The ordinary leading the extraordinary to boredom?

You said: "I will find the fishes there, naturally
They are not bound by human languages anymore
They sing inexpressible songs in perfect union all the time"

"The stopper will be pulled out from now on, everybody!
Are you guys ready?" — the lid of the coffin was opened
and the pangs returned to my abdomen
A mixture of welcome and refusal was whirling in me
You were born when I opened my eyes at last

Closed Climax

You and I are not allowed to touch each other's body anymore
The authorities fear our bodily contact will not only destroy us
but also bring chaos to the entire society — so it is forbidden

Now we have to use the power long believed as futile among the others
to establish a secret game of closeness only for two of us — first of all
a nonexistent immense tree thrusts up to the sky from the top of my head

and its leafy branches arrange an immense shadow on the ground, while
your back is split vertically in the middle and, from the opening, a hairy
four-legged beast with an adorable face is born and flops toward the tree

Nothing but the tree and the beast is seen — the animal has no habit of
drinking water and sweating — the only food it can eat is the tree's new
leaves — they are fatally toxic — clinging onto the trunk or crawling

from one branch to another, the beast keeps devouring the tree's lushness
and strips it to nothingness — now the tree looks like the little true words
I have — embracing the corpse-like cold trunk, the poison-filled animal

begins a semipermanent sleep to facilitate its own digestion and to lower
its own temperature — no more leaves to eat — no other tree to rely on
No means left for this solitary creature to get back to your split-open back

You and I are not allowed to touch each other's body anymore
Should we call this state "life"? Is it high time for us to see our
indirect touch as identical to our direct one? Nonsense? Why?

Next — a stranger is summoned from your body and so is one from mine
These two draw lots — in fact, every single citizen must do so to decide
who plays this year's sacrifice for the avoidance of the nation's fall and

who kills the victim — are they two really selected by a strange coincidence?
Isn't any jealousy-based conspiracy involved? No bias-led inequality at all?
This time my avatar has to remove yours, but next time this table may turn

Against a backdrop of a crowd keeping an unflinching eye on the ritual's
climax, my double lays its hands on the thin neck of yours — the way this
absurdity calms them down is surprising — no heroism is needed for their

despair-laden solidarity — the entire blame will be shifted to nobody else
My substitute looks into the pupils of yours and starts to strengthen its grip
While the crowd begins to vanish, the mutual joy between them two divides

their space vertically and covers it horizontally — you and I
are not allowed to touch each other's body anymore — those
who ban our contact will forget about us once their fear settles

Our secret game continues — now we are young and lively, standing together
in the center of a dance floor under a spotlight — we start swaying lightly
to Chubby Checker's full-blast voice: "Come on let's twist again like we did

last summer — round and round and up and down and go again" — as our
wriggling bodies move to each other, the distance between the two pierces us
As our fast-swinging bodies part from each other, the closeness between us is

severely felt — watching this sweating younger self of mine in its dream is
my skeleton-like self, who is lying in a coma — lying next to it while holding
its decrepit hand tightly in a coma is your skeleton-like self, naturally —

you and I are not allowed to touch each other's body anymore
Who cares — nothing can put an end to our hidden pleasures
Even if this joy is a mere illusion — our happiness never dies

Eggs and a Tower

I found a new hobby after you were gone
Every night I pull off a tablecloth quickly
from our table with some objects on it
right before I go to bed all alone

On the wrinkleless blood-colored cloth
I have put a large variety of tableware so far
for this challenge --- my delicate sense of pull
never jolted any of it whenever I tried

Last night I had a close call
I put on the cloth a hundred wineglasses
in five tiers and aimed for another success
While I closed my eyes for concentration

a sudden illusion hit me --- a giant egg
cracked and an old clock appeared from it
I was so startled I almost weakened
my elastic pull momentarily

No more last-minute visions like that
for tonight! --- I start smoothing away
the creases on the blood-colored cloth
by the window with unease when

I notice Summer gradually condensed
in the blue sky into a golden cathedral
floating aimlessly over the horizon --- what
should be placed on the table this time?

I should try the most difficult challenge
by far --- rubbing my presbyopic eyes and
having my new false teeth on my mind
I mull over as your words rise again

"Even here many kids wish to enter
the military --- maybe to escape poverty
They always die first in war --- they are
the true victims of this society!"

I break these lines and pick the following
six words --- "Kids" "Military" "Poverty"
"Die" "War" and "Victims" --- and
put them quietly on the cloth as the first tier

Autumn is now getting coagulated like ice
under the cloudy sky into a cathedral
drifting to my window with its gold
peeling off --- the tone of your words

changes --- "Enemies are your best friends
So they must remain your enemies eternally
Why do you go out of your way to join
those who kill them on the pretext of war?"

"Enemies" "Friends" "Eternally" "Kill"
and "Pretext" --- the five words I pick
for the second tier are already significant
weight for the first tier --- Winter now turns

into an edifice with its roof and walls
crumbling and wafts over the fence into
my rainy garden --- my adolescent ears
hear your voice again --- "Suppose you

get out of this town and wander alone
in the middle of nature --- can it work as
the driving force for changing this society?
Will it merely be a cowardly escape?"

"Wander" "Alone" "Nature" "Changing"
"Society" "Cowardly" and "Escape" ---
as soon as I work up the third tier
I get a cold sweat --- the entire tower

almost falls down --- now something
covers the whole surface of my window
It stares fixedly at me --- it must be
the magnificent door of the edifice ---

maybe the only relic of the lost cathedral
or the embodiment of Spring --- you speak
to me again --- "My naked body personifies
silence --- and I know nobody can dress me

but you --- should I be obedient to your choice
again today or remain naked against your wish?
This delicate voice of mine is another garment
you picked a long time ago --- remember?"

"Naked" "Silence" "Voice" and "Garment"
--- my slightly trembling infantile hands
complete the final tier when the tablecloth
holds my fingers and orders --- "Pull now"

The vital spark streams into my sweaty hands
They are about to pull the cloth resolutely
and diagonally to the floor --- is this free will
only mine? --- here comes another illusion

Your face falls off from the surface of your
head --- now a gargantuan egg is on your neck
I feel like a wanderer who searches for a song
all over the songless land the instant I pull

Ordinary Omelet

Before making love with him
she always makes omelets
to eat with him
Whenever he says to her while eating:
"I've never judged you by your appearance"
she holds her tongue

Today her omelet preparation starts as usual
First, she undresses him and begins to clean up
his neck, chest, belly,
four limbs, fingers, groin,
soles, heels, buttocks, and
every single hole

Once disjointed carefully from his shoulders
his milky arms are put on a chopping board
While they are deftly minced
he says to himself: "Her cooking and English are
still quite poor, but I will never look down
on my girl, never"

On television a throng cries for freedom
whereas they are surrounded and punished
by the brutal police force
"They look shady," he says, "but they are beautiful"
As soon as his eyeballs are winkled out
the whole chaotic image vanishes from him

The total amount of the minced arms is
far more than the two can eat
She suggests they should donate the leftovers
to those who are still suffering from hunger
What a serious facial expression
she puts on every time she says so

When she wrenches the whole legs from his torso
an impulse which has been almost
fading from his memory seizes back
vigor right in the depth of his heart
It is an urge to welcome his enemies
unconditionally, whoever they are

All the hairs on the legs are thoroughly removed
The legs are diced up from the thighs to the toes
She scoops two servings from the dices and
mixes them in a bowl
with the shredded arms
and the crushed eyeballs

"Will you use today the neck, the chest
and the belly, also?"
She answers: "I washed them just in case
but maybe no, because the intestines, the lungs
and the esophagus were too clean and tasted
awful on the last occasion"

A violent pain runs in his blood
and reminds him
again and again
of the loss of his limbs and eyes
A towel is pushed into his mouth
to stop his groan

Neither of his two favorite phrases
("We should have enough strength to
accept each other's weaknesses" and "Why
don't you wear makeup again like before?")
can be clearly pronounced anymore
She touches his groin softly and whispers:

"Unconditional love is a complete fiction
This omelet is another hard evidence of it"
She has never used his penis before: "You often

say solitude is the sole origin of happiness
Then, my dear, I believe this region is the biggest
obstacle to your happiness"

As his consciousness is being lost
anticipation for the usual smooth refined taste
rises in him all the more
A pang of guilt for forgetting all the past
and living for the moment
makes his mouth water

Her preliminaries are almost finished
She pours his tears and saliva into the pan
instead of oil
Now is the time for the highlight of her cooking
She inserts the usual elongated metal instrument
into his anus to scrape two-serving eggs from him

During her cautious extraction
the same old strange feeling buds again in him
It is an intricate mixture of guilt, self-denial, and
freedom from all responsibilities
He cannot express this feeling in words clearly
So he tries to say:

"People often say
every human being is born as
someone deeply desired, but
is it really true?"
His every word sounds like a jabberwocky
because of the towel in his mouth

Am I being killed now?
Am I being remade to survive?
Am I looking manly enough
in the eyes of this woman
looking down on me?
Am I looking adorable enough in her view?

When he reaches the zenith of his pain
she says with joy: "Finito!"
Fulfilling lovemaking awaits
right after the meal as usual
In spite of the ongoing anguish
he smiles

Sunday Double Suicide

This is a story about a tiny house you pass by everyday
Unawares — so you don't know it has four rooms and
No roof — none of the rooms is worthy of such words
As "modern" or "future" or "civilization" — will you
Wonder who lives in this old house? — will you have
Enough courage to go quietly through its small garden
Full of hydrangeas at their best and to set your foot upon
Its first room in a foolhardy explorer's way? — if so
You'll discover nobody there — instead — you'll find
An almost rotten wooden dining table — on this table
You will discover a rusty knife confronting a fossil of
Something like a pomegranate — the knife will catch
Your eye — a voice will start drifting from it: "Today's
Housework is finally over — laundry done — bathtub
Brushing done — dish washing done — garbage disposal
Done" — a different voice will be heard from the fossil:
"All we must do from now on are to burn up all the cash
And all the photos we still have and to ditch our bankbooks
And insurance cards and pensions and resident registrations
And family registers" — the knife will reply — "Besides
We must dump our ages and genders and past sexual relations
Altogether" — you will turn gloomy and shift your eyes
Into the sky — you will notice fine weather just above you
While a downpour is persisting outside — you will also
Notice a vapor trail running steadily as if it is heading for
The world's end — In the second room you will discover
Another almost rotten wooden dining table — on the table
There will be two identical small vases facing each other
One will have a pure-white flower while the other will be
Empty — a voice will leak from the flower — "From our
Family tree one male member's name has been erased —
Generating a face like his ought to have been impossible
For our blood — why was he able to be born that way?
He ended up being through with the rest of us and deported

Somewhere with his mother — nobody in my family knows
About his present whereabouts — if possible — I'd love to
Meet his descendants — I want to know why his doom
Was oriented that way — so I started on this long journey"
The flowerless vase will reply: "You got me on your way and
Addicted yourself to my titillation — you kept raping me
And I kept aborting" — the flower will answer: "Even if
You had given birth to one of those babies — I would have
Abused it to death anyway — why were you able to evolve
Out of our genealogy?" The empty vase will respond: "You
Valued the public too much and kept neglecting the private
All the time — you all were too zealous for expansion and
Growth — you all doubted that returning to this world after
Death needs enjoying nothingness before death — this sin
Led you all to create the extraordinary blood like mine" —
You will feel rather uncomfortable — your eyes will fall on
The hydrangeas in the rainy garden — you will then notice
Each tiny flower seems to see one another as its opponent
While the entire flowers look so calm and peaceful — now
You will be led smoothly to the third room — you will find
Again an almost rotten wooden dining table — two identical
Chairs will be facing each other across the table — on it there
Will be an old sepia newspaper — an article on this paper will
Feature a murderer testifying: "I did it because I was upset —
It could have been anybody" — one of the chairs will whisper:
"It could have been us" — the other will respond: "We could
Have been like this killer" — you will ask them: "What will
Start here from now?" — the two chairs will answer in unison:
"Everything will, son — why don't you make a swift decision
Before this place perishes — before somebody destroys you
And while you still remain young and beautiful?" — huh —
You'll find these chairs too musty and smelly — you won't be
Able to stand them anymore — you'll open the final door to
Meet again an almost rotten wooden dining table (and a chair)
You will also realize the table is exactly the same with the one
You bought a long time ago — you will suppress the desire to

Sit at it — on the table there will be a glass of poison to the brim
Behind the glass there will be a mirror — on its surface you will
See the clear reflections of the glass and yourself — a voice will
Come from behind the mirror: "Taking this poison is like war —
The postwar peace and reconstruction will be 100% guaranteed —
The modern history of this nation proves it!" — you'll glimpse
Behind the mirror to discover the immense summer sea — nobody
Will be on this Sunday beach — in a tide pool almost disappearing
Due to hot weather two starfishes will be in the middle of copulation
While awaiting together the next high tide — you still don't know
You may be the very high tide — moreover — you still don't know
A splendid moonbeam is now about to be reflected on the mirror
Meanwhile — again today — you'll pass by this tiny roofless
House without paying the remotest attention to it and walk away

Born in the city of Hiroshima, Japan, Goro Takano is an associate professor in the Faculty of Medicine at Saga University, Japan, where he teaches English to Japanese medical students. His past poetry collections published through BlazeVOX are *Responsibilities of the Obsessed* (2013), *Silent Whistle-Blowers* (2015), and *Non Sequitur Syndrome* (2018). *On Lost Sheep*, Takano's translation of the works of the Japanese modernist poet Shiro Murano, was published in 2017 through Tinfish (Honolulu). Takano's first Japanese-only poetry collection *Nichiyo-bi no Shinju* ("*Sunday Double Suicide*") and his second Japanese-only one *Hyaku-nen Tattara Aimasho* ("*Why Don't We Meet Again A Hundred Years Later?*") were published through Karan-sha (Fukuoka, Japan) in 2019 and 2021, respectively.

Made in the USA
Middletown, DE
09 February 2022

60850386R00050